St. Patrick's Day

by Rebecca Pettiford

Bullfrog Books

Ideas for Parents and Teachers

Bullfrog Books let children practice reading informational text at the earliest reading levels. Repetition, familiar words, and photo labels support early readers.

Before Reading
- Discuss the cover photo. What does it tell them?
- Look at the picture glossary together. Read and discuss the words.

Read the Book
- "Walk" through the book and look at the photos. Let the child ask questions. Point out the photo labels.
- Read the book to the child, or have him or her read independently.

After Reading
- Prompt the child to think more. Ask: Have you ever celebrated St. Patrick's Day? What sorts of things do you see during this festival?

Bullfrog Books are published by Jump!
5357 Penn Avenue South
Minneapolis, MN 55419
www.jumplibrary.com

Library of Congress Cataloging-in-Publication Data

Names: Pettiford, Rebecca, author.
Title: St. Patrick's Day / by Rebecca Pettiford.
Other titles: Saint Patrick's Day
Description: Minneapolis, Minnesota: Jump!, Inc., [2016] | Series: Festivals | Includes index.
Audience: Ages: 5–8. | Audience: Grades: K to Grade 3. Identifiers: LCCN 2016029352 (print)
LCCN 2016030223 (ebook)
ISBN 9781620315354 (hard cover: alk. paper)
ISBN 9781620315897 (paperback)
ISBN 9781624964893 (e-book)
Subjects: LCSH:
Saint Patrick's Day—Juvenile literature.
Classification: LCC GT4995.P3 P47 2016 (print)
LCC GT4995.P3 (ebook) | DDC 394.262—dc23
LC record available at https://lccn.loc.gov/2016029352

Editor: Kirsten Chang
Book Designer: Leah Sanders
Photo Researcher: Leah Sanders

Photo Credits: All photos by Shutterstock except: Alamy, 5, 8–9, 12–13, 14; Getty, 11, 13, 23mr; iStock, cover, 15, 23tr; Superstock, 6–7, 10; Thinkstock, 22tl, 24.

Printed in the United States of America at Corporate Graphics in North Mankato, Minnesota.

Table of Contents

Green Day 4

Symbols of St. Patrick's Day 22

Picture Glossary 23

Index 24

To Learn More 24

Green Day

It is March 17.

Today is St. Patrick's Day!

St. Patrick

St. Patrick was a Christian.

He lived in Ireland.

He told people about God.

He did good deeds.

Today, we honor Ireland and its people.

Do we have to be Irish?

No. We can all have fun!

We wear green. Why?
Green is the color of Ireland.

Oh, no!
Paul is not in green.

Molly pinches him.
Ow!

Look! It's a parade.

People dance.

They wave Irish flags.

13

Nora wears a hat.

It has a shamrock on it.

shamrock

Mr. Rob is dressed like a leprechaun.

Mom makes corned beef.
She makes cabbage. Yum!

cabbage

corned beef

We eat green cookies.
We drink green milk.

Happy St. Patrick's Day!

Symbols of St. Patrick's Day

corned beef and cabbage

Irish flag

the color green

shamrock

Picture Glossary

Christian
A person who believes that Jesus is the son of God and who follows his teachings.

leprechaun
A tricky elf from old Irish stories who some believe has hidden treasure.

corned beef
Beef that has been cured with salt; it is an Irish American food.

saint
A holy person; *saint* is often abbreviated as "St."

Ireland
An island in the Atlantic Ocean.

shamrock
A tiny green plant with three leaves that is associated with St. Patrick and Ireland.

Index

cabbage 16

Christian 7

corned beef 16

dancing 13

green 10, 11, 19

Ireland 7, 8, 10

leprechaun 15

March 4

parade 13

pinching 11

shamrock 14

St. Patrick 5, 7, 20

To Learn More

Learning more is as easy as 1, 2, 3.

1) Go to www.factsurfer.com

2) Enter "StPatricksDay" into the search box.

3) Click the "Surf" button to see a list of websites.

With factsurfer.com, finding more information is just a click away.

24